Virtual Assistant:

A guide for the Entrepreneur <u>and</u> the Virtual Assistant who are looking for one another but have no idea where to start!

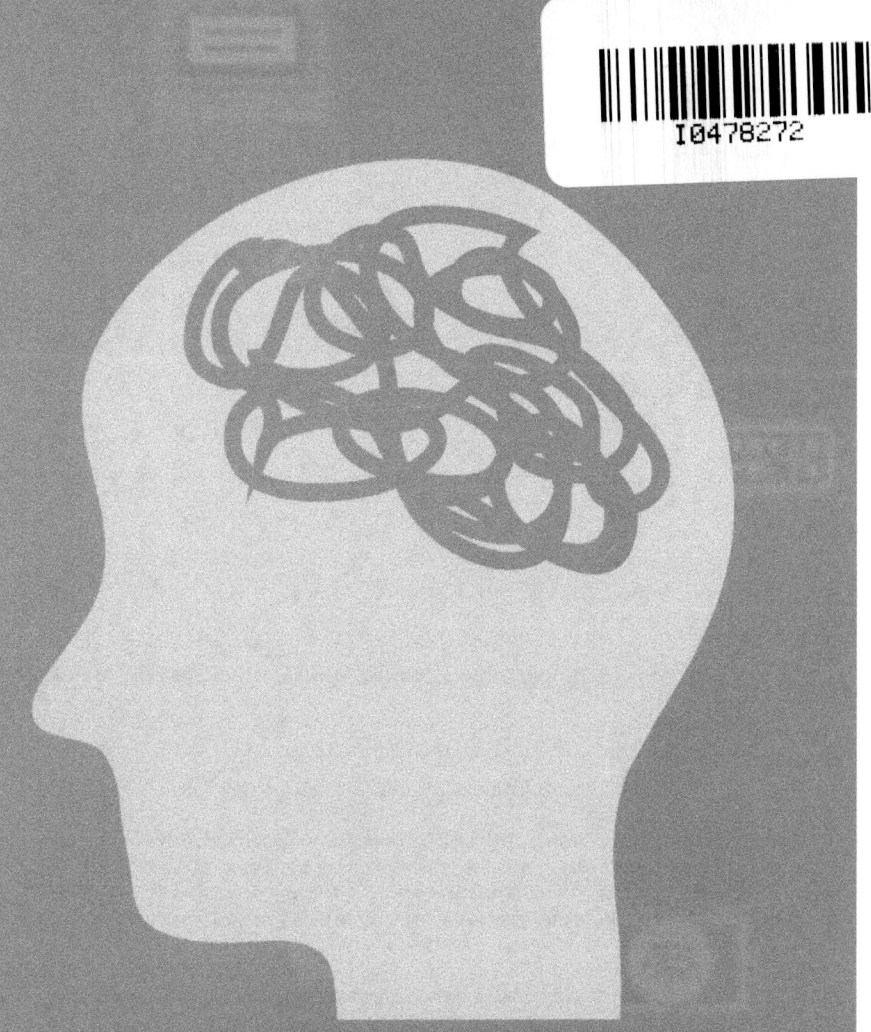

© HoJo's Teaching Adventures, LLC 2024-present. All rights reserved.

© HoJo's Teaching Adventures, LLC 2024-present. All rights reserved.

Some images used with permission from Hidey's Clipart. All rights reserved. No part of this publication may be reproduced, distributed, or transmitted in any form or by any means. This includes photocopying, recording, or other electronic or mechanical methods without prior permission of the publisher, except in the case of brief quotations embodied in critical reviews and other noncommercial uses permitted by copyright law.

No part of this product maybe used or reproduced for commercial use.

Contact the author :
www.HoJosTeachingAdventures.com/Contact

Table of Contents	Page
Chapter 1: My Virtual Assistant Story	5
Chapter 2: What Can a VA Do?	7
Chapter 3: Tips for Both Parties • Communicate • Consider a Trial Period • Have an Agreement • Handling Deadlines • Getting Approval Before Going Live • Taxes • Ending Services	8
Chapter 4: Tips for the Entrepreneur • Determining Where You Need Help • Letting Go of Control • Spending Money to Make Money • How Much Will It Cost? • How to Find a Virtual Assistant • Start Small • Before Hiring – Asking the Right Questions • Give Honest, Upfront Feedback • Ask Questions • Pay in a Timely Manner • You Don't HAVE to Give Away the Key! • Respond in a Timely Manner	12
Chapter 5: Getting Started – Entrepreneur Questions	18
Chapter 6: Tips for the Virtual Assistant • How to Find Work • When People Reach Out to You • Decide What to Charge • Communication • How to Charge? • Billing Clients • Confidentiality • Routines & Organization • Ongoing Communication • Overbooking • Just Get Started • Handling Taxes • Love Your Work! • Resources	20
Chapter 7: Getting Started – Virtual Assistant Questions	28
Chapter 8: You're Ready for Your Virtual Assistant Journey	30

© HoJo's Teaching Adventures, LLC 2024-present. All rights reserved.

Chapter 1: My Virtual Assistant Story

During the 2014-2015 school year I was working as a K-6 elementary principal of two schools and the district's K-12 special education director. However, upon my son's arrival in spring 2015 and the blood clots I developed when he was only five hours old, I knew I wouldn't be returning to the school in the fall.

That summer I began to make plans for increasing my online workload on my teaching printables and blog, as well as doing a few other side jobs online. That same summer I was approached by a friend about becoming a virtual assistant (VA) to her businesses. Not really knowing what I was getting into, I agreed and quickly found I **LOVED** the work I was doing!

Since then I've worked with over a hundred different bloggers and business owners. These have included teacherpreneurs, mommy bloggers, real estate agents, lifestyle bloggers, health entrepreneurs, and more. During this time, I've learned a great deal about the virtual assistant world! I've joined groups on Facebook specifically for virtual assistants, and read books about starting a VA business as well as many blog posts. I even wrote a VA ebook for teacherpreneurs and it has over 125 five-star reviews.

I've learned to automate as many things for myself and my clients as possible. (I'll share more of those tips throughout the book.) This ensures that I am able to stay ahead of the game and not constantly be running behind for myself or anyone else.

One of the biggest things I've learned in the last decade is that there are a LOT of people who are interested in becoming a VA, and there are just as many (if not more!) people who are interested in hiring a virtual assistant. For years, I've had people reaching out asking me for tips and ideas. That's why this book was born!

This book is meant to help the business owner who is looking for a VA and the person who is interested in becoming a VA. I'm going to share topics for both to consider. And I truly recommend you read the sections for BOTH so you are better prepared to understand where both the business owner AND virtual assistant are coming from.

Best of luck to you on your virtual assistant journey – whether you ARE the VA or you're the one hiring one. ☺

While I am an entrepreneur myself, there is no way I completely understand *your* entrepreneur journey. We are all going different directions with our business. What you currently need out of a VA and my current needs for a VA are going to be different.

With that said, I hope you love this book! If you have any questions, please feel free to reach out to me at www.HoJosTeachingAdventures.com/contact

Chapter 2: What Can a VA Do?

Are you an entrepreneur and wondering what tasks you could hire out to a virtual assistant? Or are you interested in becoming a VA but you have no idea what services you could offer? Either way, this list is for you!

- Video creation and/or editing
- Search engine optimization (SEO)
- Blog design
- Technical help on blogs
- Finding and adding affiliate links
- Email marketing
- Product editing
- Image creation
- Pinterest live pinning
- Pinterest pin scheduling
- Facebook
- Instagram
- X (formerly Twitter)
- Updating terms of use pages
- Advertising/marketing
- Media kit creation
- E-mail management
- Blogger to WordPress migration
- Taking photos of products or recipes in action
- Schedule out guest bloggers
- WordPress plugins
- Store management – Kajabi, Shopify, etc.
- Overseeing a new project or product
- Researching a new post idea or product line
- Helping with presentations
- Hotel & flight management
- Product translation
- Accounting and/or bookkeeping
- Spam comment filtering
- Watching feedback to alert you to specific reviews
- Maintain Q&A
- Keeping up with whatever you'd like while you're away or on vacation
- **AND MORE!!!** ☺

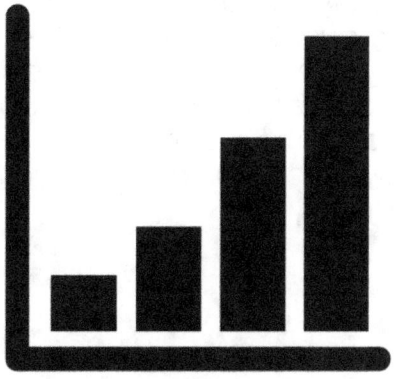

Chapter 3: Tips for Both Parties

Whether you are the entrepreneur or the virtual assistant, these tips are something to keep in mind for you both!

Communicate

Decide what type of communication you will use. Many will use e-mail and Facebook messenger for regular communication. However, texting may be another option. Setting up a monthly Skype session or a phone call to check in are other options. One client I work with set up a secret Facebook group so we can access everything at any time.

You <u>do</u> want to decide how to best communicate. If you have too many e-mails, text, Facebook messages, and other places to check – things are going to get lost in the shuffle! Decide what works best and stick with it. (I keep VA work in one email. Period. Otherwise it gets lost.)

Discuss how long the other person can expect to hear back from you. If you typically respond to messages within 24 hours, communicate that. If you are also busy teaching or working in some other fashion, share that it may take you 3-4 days to respond. Being upfront about your communication style and timeline will cause less hurt feelings down the road.

Many of the topics I discuss in this ebook are going to focus largely on communication. Whether you're the one running the business or the one helping to run it, <u>communication is HUGE!</u> As a VA I actually stopped services for one client because she would take up to six weeks to get back to me. I couldn't handle having no direction from the business owner for that long, so I parted ways. Please communicate regularly!

Consider a Trial Period

It may be in both parties best interest to do an agreed upon trial period, such as a month. There <u>are</u> going to be kinks to work out. The VA needs to find out what the entrepreneur expects and how his or her business runs. This does not come overnight. However, regular communication should ensure both parties are happy.

If things are not going well at the end of the trial period, part ways. Make sure payment has been taken care of and communicate that you will be ending. That's it. Don't make it a big deal and cause unneeded drama.

Have an Agreement

It will be in both parties best interest to have a written agreement. This can include a timeline of how long services will be provided, rates and/or retainers, confidentiality agreements, how to handle questions, and anything else that is deemed appropriate based on the type/s of services being performed.

Handling Deadlines

There are going to be times where deadlines need to be met. Agree ahead of time on how you will handle these. These agreements can even be written into the agreement mentioned on the last page. Whether a project is due the day, week, or month before, it's important for both parties to be on the same page.

The VA will need to confirm the work is done. Both parties should agree on how this will be handled. Perhaps a weekly recap e-mail is all that is necessary. If items are not completed to the entrepreneur's liking, that will need to be communicated, discussed, and fixed.

While these are all items that can be discussed before hiring ever takes place, I've found that many things come up the longer you work with someone. As long as both parties are good communicators, deadlines are typically not going to be a problem.

Getting Approval Before Going Live

There are some tasks that will need approval before going live – such as blog posts or product descriptions. How will this approval happen? Will the entrepreneur log into their blog once a week and sign off on the upcoming posts? How will they communicate this? Having a joint Google doc or Dropbox may be a great idea.

Taxes

Entrepreneurs, check with your accountant. You may have to send a 1099 to your VA if you send them over $600/year if you are based in the United States. Virtual assistants, make sure to claim the income you make! (Tax laws vary by state. I encourage you to discuss specifics with your accountant.)

Ending Services

Determine and agree ahead of time how services will end. The entrepreneur may only need VA services for a one-time project, or they may want ongoing services for an unlimited time frame. This is another area where communication is HUGE!

Please use professionalism when ending services. As big as the online world is, it's also very small. Sometimes people do not work well together, but that doesn't mean they won't work well with other people.

<u>For the Entrepreneur</u> – If your virtual assistant is no longer meeting your standards, it may be time to break ties. Or you may no longer need their help because you are going a different direction or things have changed.

If you have an end date in mind and the VA relationship has gone well, openly communicate this and determine how things will end. If you have a written agreement, go with that.

If you are ending the relationship because things are going poorly, you may want to change passwords before informing the VA.

Other things to keep in mind – have you already paid a retainer? How much money will you be losing if you end services early? These questions and more may have been addressed via the written agreement you both signed at the beginning.

<u>For the Virtual Assistant</u> – If you need to end services, let the entrepreneur know as soon as possible. Maybe your circumstances have changed and you need to cut back or end the relationship altogether. Regardless of the reason, communicate your end date. Either finish out the work you promised via the retainer <u>or</u> finish your work and send a bill.

Remain discreet and keep confidentiality in mind even after you've finished working for someone. Talking about a client – positively or negatively – may cause you to not gain more clients for fear you talk about people.

Chapter 4: Tips for the Entrepreneur

Determining Where You Need Help

Consider these things:
- What tasks do you <u>least</u> enjoy doing?
- What tasks could someone else do better than you can?

As a VA myself, I still hire services out. I can't do blog design to save my life. And while I can figure out 90% of my technical problems, they take me hours! Why should I spend hours on the project when I can pay someone a reasonable amount and they get it done in a fraction of the time?

Letting Go of Control

When determining where you need help, you also must decide what you are willing to let go of. This will vary for each person, but also keep in mind what passwords you are willing to share. You can always change them as soon as you are dissatisfied, but handing passwords to someone else can be intimidating. Yes, I know – I've done it! Letting go of control is probably the hardest thing! When I look back at my journey thus far as a online business owner, I realize I would have been so much more productive with my time if I had hired out help sooner! It's hard, but ask others who have a VA – they love the freedom it brings them!

Spending Money to Make Money

As I mentioned above, when you hire out some tasks it frees your time to do more of what you love. Whether that's more work, more time with family, or just more free time in general – how awesome would it be to do more of what you love?! If you are happier, your business is going to do better! If your business is doing better, you're going to have more money to get more help. The circle just keeps continuing, and it truly is a great thing! ☺

With the concept of spending money to make money, you may not want to choose the cheapest VA on the market. I've seen virtual assistants who charge as little as $8/hour. Many of these that I've come across are from foreign countries where English is not the native language. While I'm not saying their grammar skills are poor, do you want to take a chance that this person will use broken English in your online presence? If you do choose to go with a cheaper route, make sure you thoroughly interview the person so you don't have any unpleasant surprises pop up after they begin working for you.

How Much Will It Cost?

In the VA section of this book, I recommend the virtual assistant charge at least $20/hour – but there are some who charge $50/hour and more. It really depends on the services. Doing technical coding on a blog is harder than pinning on Pinterest. How much you spend each month is going to largely depend on what services you're looking for.

There are other VAs who work on package rates. Instead of specifically paying by the hour, you pay a set amount for a certain amount of work to be done.

You will have to determine what amount of money you are willing to invest into your business each month. A good VA will be respectful of your budget and stick to the amount you specify.

How to Find a Virtual Assistant
There are a variety of ways to find a great VA. Read the list below to see which option you are most comfortable with.

- Upwork - https://www.upwork.com/
    - I have used Upwork to fill small, one-time jobs. But I know some people have found long-term help there.
- Family or Friends
    - Do you have a family member or friend that you think would be great as a VA? Ask them to work for you! That's how I got started! I know people who have hired the stay at home mom next door, their retired parents, or even their high school or college age children. The second part of this ebook will help you and the person you want as your VA be as successful as possible together.
- Word of Mouth
    - Ask other entrepreneurs for help in finding a great virtual assistant. Some people keep pretty hush hush about hiring help, but others have no problem telling you what work they have hired out and sometimes even who they have hired.

Hiring someone with experience in the services you are seeking is nice, but its not a requirement. Keep an open mind. You want to find someone that is great for you to work with! I've personally learned that some newbies are willing to work harder than those with more experience. And training a person to do things the way I can sometimes work out perfectly.

Start Small
Like I said previously, it can be incredibly intimidating to let go control of your "baby" – aka your business. However, I am living proof that it's worthwhile!

Before Hiring – Asking the Right Questions

Before you agree to hire anyone, put them through an interview. This can be done over e-mail or messaging, but a phone call or Skype session may be best. Have a list of questions for the VA. Be upfront about what you need. If they seem hesitant or unsure, they may not be the best person for the job. However, having to train someone (like a family member or friend) may be easier than dealing with someone who lives across the country that you've never truly met.

Make sure to go with your gut feeling. There are plenty of great VAs out there. Ask around, do your own searches, and interview until you find one that is a good fit for you and your business. You don't want to have a bad experience, especially the first time around.

(If your first VA experience does go negatively, don't give up on the entire thought of a VA! This is why I recommend starting small – with a $50 or less budget and a clear deadline of what will be completed. That way you aren't out too much money, but you can see how things work and go from there.)

Give Honest, Upfront Feedback

Be upfront if something is not going the way you want it to. This is particularly useful when you first start with a virtual assistant. They don't know your expectations or exactly how your business runs. They need to hear from you to better help you.

I've had a few occasions where a client has reached out to question something I've done. It helps me better meet their needs, and a good virtual assistant will do their best to keep their client happy. And sometimes, a VA makes a mistake. (We are human after all! ☺) If the mistake is something unforgiveable – you may have to part ways. But if it's something minor, bring it to their attention so they don't repeat it.

I've found that giving feedback via screen recording to work well. (I also do this for training and pay my VA for their time to watch my video 2x over.) This way I can show what I am talking about directly on the screen for them to watch.

Ask Questions

Many times we hire a virtual assistant to do something that we are not familiar with ourselves, so it's ok to ask questions!

When I hired someone to create my WooCommerce store, I asked her more than 20 questions. She was very patient and understanding with me! Another time I asked a blog designer the same number of questions, and she got very short with me. That was my first gut feeling that something was wrong. Unfortunately I didn't trust my gut and I ended up spending more than $200 to get everything straightened out after the VA finished.

Moral of the story: Don't be afraid to ask questions!

Example questions to ask: What is the timeline for completion? How do you expect to be paid? What information to you need to access my account? How can we ensure deadlines are met? What happens if you don't meet that deadline? How will you communicate what you've done for me? Will you help me understand how to keep up maintenance on my own when you're done? And many more…

Pay in a Timely Manner

This may seem obvious to you, but please pay your virtual assistant in a timely manner. Whatever format the two of you have agreed upon, try to pay your VA within 24 hours of receiving your invoice. This tells your VA that you value them and it allows them to continue budgeting and planning for future work.

If paying quickly is not possible, ensure you pay within the deadline set up by the Service Agreement the two of you signed. If something comes up where you will be away or paying late, communicate that! Most VAs are very understanding about your circumstances, but they also rely on that income for their day-to-day living.

You may worry that your VA is going to somehow hurt your business, but they worry that you're going to have them do a bunch of work and then not pay them. It's no fun for either party.

You Don't HAVE to Give Away the Key!

You've worked hard to build your business up to what it currently is. Handing someone you hardly know the keys to everything is a scary thought!

Yes, you may need to do more legwork upfront to get things organized if you don't want to hand over the key to some aspect of your business. It's your call what you're comfortable with, but just know that it **IS** possible to get help with your business without putting everything on the line.

If you love your VA and trust them 110%, hand over those keys! It's one less thing for you to have to think about! ☺

You can also consider a password sharing program like LastPass.

Respond in a Timely Manner

Respond to any questions your virtual assistant asks in a timely manner. If your VA typically gets back to you within 24 hours, do your best to give them the same courtesy. They are working a business just as you are, and you should be respectful of their time. Remember, they may end the VA services if they are unhappy with you – so you do not want to lose a VA you love!

This does not mean you can't go on vacation or enjoy your weekends unplugged! If you're going to be away from your computer for an extended period of time, or if you always take Sundays completely off – communicate that! This will allow your VA to know what to expect from you.

Chapter 5: Getting Started – Entrepreneur Questions

There are a lot of factors to consider when hiring a virtual assistant. These questions are meant as a starting point for you to consider as you determine what services to have a virtual assistant provide and how to continue on your journey.

- Are you willing to let go of control?
- How much work do you want to hire out?
- What tasks do you want (or need) to hire out?
- Do you want to hire someone on a trial basis? How will this look? What will you do if the VA is not a good fit?
- What passwords and information are you willing to share with your VA? (Pinterest? Facebook? Instagram? X? Newsletter? E-mail? Blog? Others?)
- How much are you willing to spend each month to help grow your business? Where will you direct this money being spent? (Some people hire more than one VA to each do a different task.)
- Who do you want to hire? Another entrepreneur? A virtual assistant outside of your niche? A former teacher, turned stay-at-home mom? Your neighbor? Your college age child? The possibilities are endless!
- What questions will you ask when interviewing a VA? How will you conduct the interview? Via Skype? E-mail? Phone?
- If you choose to hire someone you know who doesn't fully understand the business, how will you train them?
- How will you provide feedback to your VA? What will you do if things aren't going the way you expected?
- How will services end with your VA? Did you hire them for a one-time project, or do you need ongoing services? This may have been included in the written agreement.
- How will you pay your virtual assistant? PayPal? Check? Stripe? Freshbooks? Zelle?

- How often will you be able to respond to your VAs questions? How will you let your VA know your anticipated response time?
- What timeframe are you looking at? Do you need a one-time project, or are you wanting ongoing support? How will you communicate this with your VA?
- What will your deadlines look like? Do you want projects a day, week, or month before you go live with them? How will you communicate this with your virtual assistant?
- How do you want the VA to communicate when they complete tasks? What will you do if items are not completed to your liking?
- How will you communicate with your virtual assistant/s? What timeline will you have for responding to messages?
- Do you need a written agreement before work begins? What do you expect to be in the agreement? (And what will you do if your VA does not provide those items?)
- How will you handle tax obligations? Do you have an accountant to help?

There are a variety of other questions you may want to consider before hiring a virtual assistant. Think about your situation, the services you currently provide through your business, and determine what other questions you may have.

Chapter 6: Tips for the Virtual Assistant

How to Find Work

You can join a site like www.upwork.com

Do a search on Facebook for Virtual Assistant groups. I used to belong to a few when I was first looking for clients and it helped!

If you are specifically looking to be a VA for a specific niche, let your friends know. Post about it in those niche groups if that is allowed.

You may want to set up a blog, website, or Facebook page for your business.

Do you have friends who are VAs? Reach out to them. See if they might refer people to you if their client list is currently full.

Please know that it can take awhile to find consistent work. I started with one client in June 2015, and that was the only steady client I had for over two months.

During this time, pick up small, misc. jobs. You never know when getting paid to proofread one item may lead to a steady position with someone. Or they may speak highly of you to a friend!

When People Reach Out to You

When someone reaches out to you, be ready! You may want an application or checklist for future clients. Know what your strengths and weaknesses are so you can clearly articulate what services you are comfortable doing and what you're willing to learn.

Be upfront with them. If you've never touched a newsletter before (or whatever it is they are requesting), say so! It's better to be upfront with them than upset them and cause yourself to have a bad reputation.

Decide What to Charge

Deciding what to charge for VA services can be tough! I've seen people charge as little as $8/hour and even up to $120/hour for specialized services. I'm sure there are even more extremes, but that's simply what I've noticed in the last few years.

Keep in mind that you <u>will</u> need to turn your income into the IRS. Many accountants tell their clients that they should be sending out a 1099 to anyone who makes over $600/year. The government is going to take roughly 1/3 of your check right off the top. So if you only charge $15, that leaves you with $10 an hour, before expenses.

You may also find it helpful to do a little math. If you currently have an online ecommerce site making $800/month while only putting in 10 hours each week – that means you are making $20/hour. Why would you charge anyone less than that when you could be spending that time on your own store and blog?

One of the first virtual assistant coaches I started following says to always charge at least $20/hour. It will largely depend on what services you are providing. Doing the technical, behind the scenes work on a blog is worth more money than Pinterest simply because almost anyone can pin – but it takes more knowledge and expertise to do coding and design work.

Here's another option to consider – particularly as you become more proficient with your virtual assistant work… You can create various packages for your clients to choose from.

- <u>Benefits of Packages</u> – You no longer have to track your time, you simply do the work. If you are wanting to expand your business and hire associates, it easier to pay them per package. Invoicing can be faster.
- <u>Drawbacks of Packages</u> – If a project takes longer than you expected, you are getting paid less per hour.

I do <u>not</u> recommend starting with packages if you are a new VA. It took me nearly 18 months of being a VA to know how long various projects took me. Only at that time was I able to create a fair package price that reflected the time I put in.

Communication

Decide how communication will look on your end so you can be upfront about this from the very beginning. Set and communicate your working hours. I prefer all contacts to come through e-mail because I can keep up with them easier. But some clients prefer Facebook messenger.
I promise to get back to clients within 24 hours. I give them all of this information upfront so they know what to expect. Also determine how you will let your clients know if you are going on vacation or will be away from the computer for an extended amount of time. This way they know ahead of time and aren't blindsided by you being gone. (But make sure you have everything taken care of that should be!)

Because I kept strong communication with all my clients, I was able to take off about three months of maternity leave from February-April 2017 when my daughter was born. I did do some work during that time, but for the most part all projects were completed ahead of time.

How to Charge?

Now that you know how much to charge, you need to determine how you're going to set up your time. You may choose to bill clients at the end of the month after you've performed the work, or you may have them pay ahead through a retainer.

Make sure you have a plan in place for a client who pays late or doesn't pay you at all. You may want to charge a late payment fee or pursue legal action.

If you use a retainer, decide what you will do if your client does not use (or you're unable to finish) all the hours within that retainer. You may have the hours carry over from one month to the next.

Know how you will bill clients. Some use 15 minute increments, while I literally track each minute I work since I have two little ones underfoot who may need me at a moment's notice.

Determine all of these things ahead of time. It is also a good idea to include this information in the written agreement you and your client both sign off on.

Billing Clients

There are a variety of ways to bill your clients. Here are a few options.

If you have a business account on PayPal, you can invoice people that way. Just keep in mind that PayPal may charge a fee for this.

Another option is to directly e-mail your clients an invoice. You can do an online search for plenty of other invoice options as well. After your clients get the invoice they can send you money via PayPal, Zelle, or another agreed upon method.

You could also use programs like Freshbooks, Harvest, or 17Hats.

There are many other options available for billing. If you know of one or hear about one from someone else, look into it to see if it will fit your needs.

Confidentiality

My recommendation is to <u>never</u> tell others who your clients are. It may make your clients uncomfortable if you are talking about them in any way. If you need a reference, ask your client if they are comfortable providing one that you can use on your blog or website. Or even ask both parties if they would mind talking to one another, but make sure they both agree before you share any names.

Including a confidentiality agreement within your virtual assistant contract can be a great tool! You could have one on hand to share with potential clients as further proof that you are a professional. It will help with peace of mind.

Routines & Organization

Keeping organized is key to being a great virtual assistant! While doing this for one client can be relatively easy, it gets more challenging as you add more clients. It may be best to start with one client, get some great routines and documents in place, and then add more people to your clientele list.

My recommendation is to automate as many processes as you can. I have used many different programs in my time as a VA – Tailwind to schedule Pinterest, Hootsuite and SmarterQueue for social media, and even just a simple Google spreadsheet.

To help me get everything done each day, I have a daily to do list. That way I can cross things off each day. I also have a list of things that I need to get done within the week.

Ongoing Communication

As your work continues with a client, you're going to have questions. It may be appropriate to e-mail them immediately to get clarification. Or it might make sense to set up phone or Skype conversations every other week or once a month. Find a system to track the questions you have. This way you are ready with all of your questions whenever you meet with a client.

Overbooking

Know how many hours you have in a day or week to devote to your clients. You don't want to overbook yourself. If one client wants you to schedule 20 pins a day, it's important to know about how long that will take you. This will take some doing, but figuring how long each task takes does come with time.

Have a plan in place in case you accidentally overbook yourself. Perhaps you'll offer a discount, or you may be able to outsource your work to help save time (if your client is ok with this and it's in your contract). If overbooking does occur, figure out a solution so it won't happen again.

Just Get Started

Becoming a virtual assistant can be hard work. There is a lot to know, learn, and do! You're not going to figure it all out overnight, but don't let that stop you! Just get started! Do NOT let fear of the unknown paralyze you!

It may take you awhile to find clients. It may take you even longer to really know what you're doing, but that's alright. If you want to be a virtual assistant – go for it! Work hard, figure things out along the way, keep communication open with your clients, and make the most of it!

Want to get a jump start on being a VA? Reach out to an online business person or entrepreneur buddy. Tell her that you are starting a VA business. Offer to edit a product, create some images, or something else for a reduced price or even for free. In exchange for your services, ask for honest feedback on how you're doing and any ideas for improvement. This person may also be able to refer you to future clients, *become* a future client, or give you a referral for your portfolio.

Make sure this person knows you are learning this for free or at a discount for a short time. You deserve to be compensated, so do NOT work for free or at a discounted rate for long!

Handling Taxes

You will most likely need to claim any VA money you make. I track everything throughout the year via Freshbooks, Microsoft Word, Excel, or a Google Spreadsheet. Then I send my income and expenses to my accountant at tax time. It's pretty painless. Talk to your accountant about laws in your state.

You may also be able to claim deductions for your business. Again, talk to your accountant. Mine allows me to deduct a portion of my internet bill, cell phone bill, and my home office. See what you may be able to deduct.

Love Your Work!
I don't know your personal story, but think about why you are wanting to become a virtual assistant. Perhaps your family needs help paying the bills. Or may you're just wanting a little extra spending money. Even still, maybe you're looking at this as your new full-time career.

Your answer will determine how you handle your business, how much it grows, and how much you love it. For me personally, I started being a VA to help pay the bills – but I soon realized that being a VA in the real estate niche was not for me. I let go of a six-month client and decided to pursue teacherpreneurs because I like the field of education and understand it better. Since then I've come to *love* my virtual assistant work!

Resources
These are tools that have helped me keep organized within my virtual assistant business.
- Tailwind (scheduling Pinterest)
- Hootsuite (scheduling various social media)
- Stock Unlimited (to make graphics)
- Deposit Photos (more stock graphics)
- You can see even more of an updated list of resources I use in my business here - www.hojosteachingadventures.com/teacherpreneur-resources

Chapter 7: Getting Started – Virtual Assistant Questions

There are many things to consider before starting as a virtual assistant. Don't get me wrong, you can just start and figure it out as you go. (That's what I did!) But if you're wanting a few more guidelines and questions to help you get started, that's where this list comes into play!

Use these questions as a starting point of things to consider as you get started. More questions may come up as you go, but this will be a great starting point.

- What tasks can you do? What tasks do you <u>want</u> to do? (Yes, there is a difference.)
- How much will you charge your clients? Will this be hourly or based on packages you create?
- How will you advertise and find work?
- What will your working hours be? How will you let your clients know this? How will you communicate when you are going on vacation or being away from the computer for an extended period of time?
- Will you bill clients at the end of the month after you've performed the work, or will you have them pay ahead to hold a retainer?
- If you bill at the end of the period and your client skips the bill or pays late, how will you handle that? A late payment fee? Will you pursue legal action if they still don't pay?
- If your client pays via a retainer and you don't use all of the hours, how does that work? Will those hours carry over?
- Will you bill by the minute? 15 minute increments? Have all of this determined ahead of time so you know what to tell your clients.
- How will you bill your clients? PayPal? Another program? Will you create your own invoices or use the ones within the program you choose?
- What forms of payment will you accept? Zelle? PayPal? Stripe?

- How will you communicate with your clients? What timeline will you have for responding to client questions and answers?
- Do you want to start on a trial basis? How long will this trial be? What will you do if you don't feel the client is a good fit?
- Do you need a written agreement? Find a template online and edit it to best fit your needs. Make sure to edit it to best reflect the needs of each client as they come.
- How will you communicate that everything is done? What will you do if the entrepreneur does not like what you've done or asks you to redo it?
- How will you handle tax obligations? Do you have an accountant to help? What deductions can you claim?
- How will services end with a client? Were you hired on a one-time project, or did the person need ongoing services? This may have been included in the written agreement.
- Are you prepared for the first client who reaches out to you? Will you have them complete an application?
- How will you handle confidentiality?
- How will you stay organized? How will you handle multiple clients?
- How will you communicate with clients as you continue doing work with them? Will some problems need immediate answers while others can wait for a weekly or monthly check in? How will you handle each one?
- How will you ensure you don't overbook yourself? How will you determine how many hours you can work in a week?
- If you do happen to overbook yourself and are unable to complete something within the time you specified, what will you do? Will you offer your client a discount? What else could you do?

Think about other questions you may have for your clients (or yourself). Be prepared for more questions to surface the longer you do virtual assistant work. Your clients' needs will change and new questions come up. That's perfectly normal!

You're Ready for Your Virtual Assistant Journey

Whether you are hiring your first virtual assistant or starting your VA business, you're ready!

You've learned my story, what a VA can do, tips for both the entrepreneur AND the virtual assistant, plus even more.

Take what you've learned and get started!

www.HoJosTeachingAdeventures.com

Heather Jo aka HoJo
© HoJo's Teaching Adventures, LLC

All rights reserved. Purchase of this unit entitles the purchaser the right to reproduce the pages in limited quantities **for single classroom or home use only**. Duplication for an entire school, an entire school system, friends, neighbors, or commercial purposes is strictly forbidden without written permission from the publisher.

Copying **any** part of this product and placing it **on the Internet in any form (even a personal/classroom website)** is **strictly forbidden** and is a violation of the Digital Millennium Copyright Act (DMCA). These items can be picked up in a Google search and then shared worldwide for free.

www.ingramcontent.com/pod-product-compliance
Lightning Source LLC
Chambersburg PA
CBHW030045230526
45472CB00005B/1684